LET IT OUT

Book Design by HMDPUBLISHING

Over the last couple of years, I have experienced my ups and downs in this life. The book is dedicated to all who have been a part of my roller coaster. You may not have known it before, but I want you to know that your smiles, hugs, encouragement, and love for me are why I am still alive today. I type this dedication out as a person who has overcome suicide not because of my strength but because of the Lord's strength. And He's ability to move through people to help impact my life. God has used many of you to impact my life in such a way that helped me see I have a reason to live. So, thank you! Thank you for your love. Thank you for being part of my story! I love taking this time to write my first book. I hope to be back writing another one. Until we meet again, God bless you all, and I love you from the bottom of my heart……

Contents

Daddy Issues

"Some people weren't wicked; they were just weak."

- Bishop Mayceo Smith

One of the heartbreaking aspects of life is knowing that you have a parent, somebody who is supposed to be your leader and mentor. Somebody to teach you lessons and prepare you for whatever life brings. Somebody who is supposed to love, care, and encourage you. Then look at your life and realize that you don't have that! That was my reality with my father. He wasn't there for the first time I scored in a game. He wasn't around when I first preached or graduated high school or college. He was not there to pick me up when I was down. He was not there to wipe away the tears. And quite frankly, it sucked. Sometimes, I wanted to call or even get in his face and ask questions like; how can you give birth to somebody and never be there for them? How could you birth a child and then run away from the child? What did I do to you for you to walk out like that? Do you understand the hurt that you caused me? Do you know how badly you affected me? I don't think you do!

When I was around 2 or 3, my first memory of him came to my head, and I often think about it sometimes. It was him hitting my mother. Imagine being that young and seeing something like that. It would have a significant effect on you mentally. And to find out my mother wasn't his first victim that he did that to really hurt me a lot. You're supposed to be a man, yet you put your hands on women. In my mind, he was weak to me. I held on to anger for him for years. I pretended everything was okay when I saw him, but deep down inside, I just wanted to punch him and walk away. This may sound like I'm bad-mouthing my father, but I want you to understand how inconsistent and hypocritical this man is and how he was never a man of his word. Nor do I think he understood the effect he had on me.

I questioned God about the situation. I couldn't have gotten a different parent? What was the whole point of this non-relationship? Why give me somebody who had no desire to be there? I really could never make sense of it, and to make matters worse, seeing my siblings grow up with two parents in the house hurt me even more.

Being young was hard because little kids are naive to things like this. No matter how often he didn't show up when I was younger, the disappointment lasted once I was told, "I would see you the next time." The same hope I had as a younger kid drifted away quickly as I got older. The hurt of seeing my siblings with their father went away because there was no point in dwelling on that, but it did make me hate him even more. The anger was fired up within me, and I didn't care to ever speak to him again. I was tired of feeling like the one who caused the damage in the relationship. I was done faking like everything was okay when he eventually came around. I was done with it all.

Abandonment issues

When I hear a black kid talk about having their biological father in their lives and living in the home,

I always say this dark-humor joke I came up with. "Oh wow, you know your father?". Almost every time I say it, everybody around me laughs and says, "Bro, what is wrong with you?". If you have a sense of humor, you will find it funny; otherwise, you will probably think something is seriously wrong with me. I tend to make jokes out of my pain, so you will have to excuse me for that. If it comes down to it, I think I could have an excellent career if I chose to do comedy. But the stereotype that black fathers are nonsexist in their child's life is, in fact, true. In 2020, one study showed that mother-only households accounted for 44% of Blacks. That was more than any other race; the next closest was 24%. This may be due partially to deaths or even incarceration, but it doesn't help the case at all. What it highlights is that if you are black and you are reading this book, there is a high likelihood that you didn't have your father in your life and are feeling the same emotions as me.

You have asked the same questions in your mind that I mentioned earlier. You felt the same anger. Deep down inside, you want to scream in their face because they don't even realize what they have done to you. You don't even know what effect not having your father in your life had on you. There is a thorn on your side, but you are so numb to the thorn that you don't know it is affecting your everyday interactions.

You want to know the real reason why you don't trust people. You want to know why you don't allow anybody in. You don't believe people are who they say they are because of the parental issues you experienced in life. Because these are all early childhood issues, they can easily be unnoticed now that you are a teenager or an adult. The toxic traits you now carry, you can't even notice how much damage it's causing to some excellent relationships you should be having because you are "guarding yourself." Memories don't just go away; they are stored deep in our brains and become our triggers for actions later in life. Your cycles of being in and out of relationships are because of a hole in your heart.

My relationship with him affected many others, and I didn't even know it. That relationship played a part in my romantic relationships, friendships, and my most important relationship, the one with God. When it comes to all these relationships, I have difficulty allowing people into my heart because I don't think they will stay around for long. I wasn't wrong about that, but partially, I was wrong. There are some relationships that God gives us that are for a season, and then there are some that God gives us that are long-lasting. But I was blind to the long-lasting ones. I let abandonment beat me up. It lied to me every day, telling me not to allow this person or that person in. When people asked me to open up, it told me not to. Abandonment brought fear and caused me to hurt people because I was hurting and afraid that they would hurt me. Abandonment caused me to feel depressed and left me insecure. It made me second guess if I am worthy enough to be in somebody's life. Abandonment clogged my mind, convincing me that if my father didn't love me correctly, what makes you think somebody else would be able to? And I started to believe it. That thought was always in my mind, even when I sat in rooms with people laughing and having fun. Even as I had some fantastic moments with family and friends, abandonment was stalking me every step of the way, ripping me of true love and joy that was right in front of me. My problem was that I was listening to abandonment and not the truth.

The truth was, ***"A friend loves at all times, and a brother is born for adversity" (Proverbs 17:7 NKJV).*** I let one loss (that wasn't a loss) affect my relationships. I didn't realize that was my problem until I was 20. I was

"Memories don't just go away; they are stored deep in our brains and become our triggers for actions later in life."

closed off while faking like I loved being around people. I was all smiles, but I felt that relationships would always be temporary for me. Ecclesiastes 4:9 says, "***Two are better than one because they have a good return for their labor***" (NIV). I could not fully see the gift in these verses since I am still stuck on that particular hole in my life.

My relationship with God was suffering a lot as well. Because my early father was inconsistent, I instantly assumed that God would be the same way. It was hard to comprehend that He told me He would never leave or forsake me. Any time I made a mistake, I thought God had rejected me. I believed that God was so far away from me that I could not find my way back to Him. But I was wrong, and so are you. To think that God who is love (1 John 4:8) would not be love is ridiculous. He has expressed His love from the beginning of time. He didn't just give to the people who did right by blessing them. He also showed it to the disobedient, unfaithful, and backsliders by providing grace and mercy. But with so much hurt by our earthly relationships, our viewpoint of Christ has completely shifted from the Word. How do you and I get back to being focused again? By addressing the hole in our hearts.

"He is a father to the fatherless" (Psalms 68:5)

What hole in your life do you think you are blind to? Are you sitting at the end of the bed in disbelief and hurt that your parent wasn't the parent you wanted? Are you hot-boxing in the car or drinking off the pain of abandonment? Are you pushing your pain to the side like it is nothing? Or are you bleeding out on people because you have trust issues? Whichever one you are doing, it is time to face the pain. This pain is holding us back, and it's time to face the fact that the pain is weighing us down. I mean, heck, we already focus on the negative. So, let's not focus on the negative; that would only give negativity power over us. For us to win, though, we have to do something significant!

Forgiving them is best for me.

We are holding on to this pain because of one word: unforgiveness. I won't get into details nor say who out of respect. But I see people in my family who have never let go of the hurt of the past be pulled by it daily. They're mentally locked in a chokehold from their past that has poisoned their actions. Unforgiveness is like holding your breath but hoping your enemy suffocates instead. Our inability to forgive does nothing to the person that has hurt us. It weighs us down. It builds walls that block off any and everybody. It keeps you second-guessing anybody that comes into your life. Somebody once told me they get afraid when something is too good because now they expect the worst to happen. I had thought that before, but hearing somebody say it out loud to me was shocking. Then it hit me. You cannot fully enjoy life with bitterness in your heart. Bitterness is the fruit produced from the seed of unforgiveness.

It doesn't matter what area of your life you are bitter about. If bitterness is in you, it will haunt you until you do something about it. People can tell that something is bothering you just by your actions. You can lie and say it doesn't bother you anymore, but I guarantee your energy will change if who hurt you walks into the room. Your anger and outbursts will speak to it all and stink up the room. You can go to church and worship, then leave, and by the end of the day, you are back to feeling the hurt. You can do all the self-care in the world, but you will only have proper self-care once you look unforgiveness in the face. Forgiving is not for the enemy that hurt you but for you.

One day, my Bishop talked about forgiveness and said, "***Some people weren't wicked; they were just weak.***" That part hit me. It made me think about how weak my father must have been because he didn't have his birth father around. Even though he had a father figure in his life, one full of love, wisdom, and kindness, he was focused on being abandoned by his birth father. That darkness sat with him day and night. It sat in him so long that he turned his back on the people who loved him and left his kids, whom he was supposed to love. Do you see the trend? It started with his pain that created a cycle. A cycle that caused him to drift away from his responsibilities. Upon gaining a new perspective, I was able to grasp this concept better. My father wasn't hurting me intentionally; his actions were consequences of hurt being inflicted on him. And now he was unknowingly passing the same pain onto me. A famous saying goes, "Hurt people hurt people," and that couldn't be truer for people in situations like mine. I am not excusing the behavior; I am simply saying that once you understand this concept, it eases the pain gradually.

At the same time, I received this revelation; I was experiencing other draining things in my life, and I knew I needed to talk to somebody about everything. That's when I realized that if I don't do something about this, I will allow my future to be filled with darkness and suffer the same effect that he suffered. So, I decided to seek counseling.

The meetings went well. I found the root of all my problems after about a month. While sitting in one of my meetings with my counselor, she asked me about my support system that I have had. I listed people like my mom and grandparents at first. But I dug deeper and began to think about my mentors, teachers, and coaches throughout my life. My counselor told me, "Do not focus on what isn't there but rather on what is there." I was looking at that one dark hole and not focusing on what was around me. When I focused on the fact that I had people who loved me and on the truth that I had father figures in my life, such as my stepdad and grandfather, I could let go of what once held me captive. It takes time to overcome darkness, but the more you allow light to shine on darkness, the more darkness has to tremble. Those words from my pastor resonated in my heart. It helped me let go of the hurt I carried around all my life.

My counselor had me write a letter I would want to give to my father. I wrote it, came to the meeting, and read it aloud. After that, she took me to the shredder, and we put the letter there. It felt good, too. It felt great to let go of all I had stored up. It was like I was attending a funeral that I was longing for. This is weird to say because nobody longs for a funeral. Yet, it was needed and refreshing. I was glad I opened up to somebody and allowed them to help me.

Now, I know how my people feel about talking to counselors. I will dive into this topic in later chapters, but I want to set the tone early, so hear me out. I'm speaking to everybody, but I need the people of my culture actually to receive what I'm about to say. You must clear your hearts from past beliefs and listen openly. It would help if you talked to a professional. Talking to your family and friends will only sometimes work. You may run into getting advice from a hurt person with guarded opinions. You need somebody trained to work with these types of issues. They have been gifted by God Himself with this type of work.

Don't avoid it because this is exactly what you need. It is a life changer. As they say, we need Jesus and somebody's couch to discuss everything we hold on to. I guarantee you that when you take that step to seek counsel, you will find that you have some baggage you need to get rid of. The question is not why are you afraid to talk to this stranger, but are you embarrassed to face your baggage? My only reason for writing this book is to let out all my baggage while also making you comfortable enough to say, "I can let mine out as well." While we continue to look through my bag, look through yours and see what needs to be let out.

QUESTIONS TO ASK SELF

1. What from how you parents treated you as a child still hurts you?

2. What hole in your heart do you need to heal?

3. Who from your past do you need to forgive? Why is it so hard for you to forgive that person?

4. Why are you embarrassed to face your baggage? What could be some positives to unbagging your issues?

I AM NOT MY THOUGHTS

"You don't have to control your thoughts. You just have to stop letting them control you."

- ***Dan Millman***

We have all heard the expression, "Your mind is a terrible thing to waste," which is true. Some people think about the brain when talking about the mind, but they are two different elements. Our brains are physical organs, whereas the mind is the part that's aware of everything surrounding us, shaping our thoughts and feelings, also known as our consciousness.

There are three parts of the mind. The first part is called the conscious mind. This is the place where we're aware of things and think. The conscious mind can be easily persuaded or manipulated. It changes based on an argument that can be happening externally or internally. The second part of the mind is the unconscious mind. This part is the creator of dreams. Here, all sorts of ideas, issues, and events are stored in the memories of things that happened throughout our days. The third part (and the part I want to focus on) is the subconscious mind. This part of our minds stores every moment of our lives and influences our behaviors based on what we endured in the past. The worst part about this area is that we don't even notice that we may act a certain way due to our subconscious mind.

Pretty scary, right? Our goal is to stop living in that space and learn to live in the moment of now. For us to get there, we have to revisit the past. We must clean out our subconscious mind, which is holding files and manipulating our movement. So, take a moment and reflect on your life. Jot down some stuff and think about the darkest days you've experienced. As uncomfortable as it may be, this will be very important. You may not want to do this exercise, but trust me. It is beneficial to your future! Your actions now are because of some moment from your past. So, you can take a break from reading and return when you've done the exercise.

Now that you have revisited those moments, can you connect them to something in your history that triggered you to move like that? I understand if you can't think of a connection now, but there's one. The evidence is there. Triggers happen not because of the present-day issue but because of traumatic past events. Anger expressed on the outside is depression living on the inside. Anger is the bullet shot out from the gun of depression that was triggered! The present rage or anger may indicate that whatever is happening now has caused you pain and annoyance. If you find yourself constantly reacting defensively, it's likely a defense mechanism constructed as a result of your past trauma.

You respond defensively to avoid feeling powerless or being mistreated again. You probably are always argumentative, not because you love to debate (sometimes I do love to discuss) but because people for the longest told you that you were wrong when you had the evidence that you were right. Whatever it is, your past is driving your actions right now! Insecurity, doubt, fear, worry, anger, or jealousy got you wrapped around its finger, and you don't even know! That may have been hard to hear, but it's the truth. Your subconscious mind is winning, poisoning your thoughts and actions, causing you to engage in a mental war. My friend, I am here to tell you you're not alone in this war. I have been there, and I'm still fighting against my thoughts. But I have learned over time how to tune down my thoughts more and more. It took a minute to know this, but I began seeing my life was affected based on my thoughts, and that's when it started to make sense.

What are you listening to?

The more you listen to something, the more you will become just like it. That became my reality day by day. It wasn't external voices feeding me lies but internal voices. I can proudly say that many people have spoken positive affirmations about my life (for which I am grateful). But nobody noticed the internal voices that spoke against every positive affirmation from people and the word of God. In Ephesians 6:12 (TPT), the Bible says, "***Your hand-to-hand combat is not with human beings, but with the highest principalities and authorities operating in rebellion under the heavenly realms. For they are a powerful class of demon-gods and evil spirits that hold this dark world in bondage"***. My fight wasn't happening against humans. It was the internal wars that waged day and night.

I lost a plethora of battles within my mind daily. To be honest, I've been a prisoner of my thoughts throughout most of my college years. It was hard for anybody to tell, though, because I still showed up with a smile, did my best, and walked confidently. But I was trapped in my mind. I couldn't escape for the longest. For days, my mind just raced with thought after thought after thought. It sucked because it didn't matter where I was or what I was doing; I was not living life! I was trapped in my mind while life was passing by. When I woke up, thoughts were waiting. And when I hit the pillows, they begin to race. The thoughts were there even when I was with family, around friends, and even in church. My thoughts had so much power over me that I became my enemy. I hate to admit it, but it's true. Although I've been growing and accomplishing things like graduating college and finding good jobs. I noticed I would tend to focus on the negative more than the positive. Doing this has not been suitable for my thought process. By focusing on the negative over the positive, I'd trained myself (without trying to teach myself this way) to search for all the negatives and have a reason to complain.

There's no joy in this. I see why the Bible tells us not to complain. It makes me feel like [expletive]. I had good things going on. But I couldn't enjoy them because of my complaining spirit. I would beat myself up over mistakes and listen to the lies that told me, "I'll be nothing" or "I'll always find a way to mess things up; what a mistake!" I never took the time to celebrate my accomplishments or how far I have come because I was too busy focusing on something I needed to improve or a mistake I made. I was like the man in Mark chapter 5 cutting himself up with laws.

The question I was left facing was how did I get here? When and where did I allow myself to come kneeling to these lies? How did I let these thoughts gain authority over me?

The enemy's game

I hate to admit this, but the enemy is a little clever. He still loses the battle, but that doesn't stop him from roaming ***"around like a roaring lion, looking for someone to devour" (1 Peter 5:8 GNT)***. Peter uses an interesting animal to describe the devil. A lion! Instantly, you might think about being the king of the jungle, but that's not what the Bible says. The devil is no king. What Peter does, though, is describe how the enemy hunts. When a lion is hunting, they tend to prefer the weaker animals. They also thrive at hunting in the cover of darkness, where they can stalk their prey without being noticed. That is exactly how the enemy hunts. He waits until we are in a weak, dark place, then jumps on us to devour us.

My weak place was my sin. My dark place was my depression. It started with the fragile place that led me to my dark place. I was unaware of my weakness but not the enemy. He studied me every day until he found my one flaw: self-control! Once he noticed my flaw, he began tempting me. Let me say this for those who always look to blame the enemy for their mistakes because I believe that we give the enemy too much credit. The enemy can only tempt you but not force you to do anything. Partaking in the temptation is your choice. Jesus and Satan were in the wilderness for 40 days and 40 nights. Jesus was only tempted. Satan never took Jesus' hand and forced Him to do anything. You decide in those split seconds to give in or not.

I failed the test of being tempted over and over again. Did I turn away from falling into temptation? No! I wasn't aware of my weakness then, so it was easier to fall into it. But at some point, I had to stop and ask myself how we keep falling for the same little trap. That's when I prayed for God to expose me to my weakness. I needed to know my faults and knew that if I prayed to God, He would show me. A lack of self-control caused me to stumble into my sin. My lack of self-control did not come alone by itself, however. With it came lust, and with that came a feeling of "needing" to feel wanted. Do you see the pattern? When flaws come, they come in bunches, not just by themselves. My issue had roots that then grew a plant that produced unwanted fruits.

Even after my fault came to light, I still somehow fell into the enemy's trap now and then. I would beat myself up over this because I knew better. I knew I wasn't supposed to be lying in bed with this girl, but I still did it. I knew I was supposed to be single, but I called all the wrong people because my desire for affection was high. I knew it was better for me to shut up and let somebody talk, but I just had to respond. I gave into temptation not because I liked it (even though it felt good at that moment) but because I let it become a routine. Falling into temptation can look less like a trap and more like a habit if we become comfortable with it.

In 1st Corinthians 6, Paul speaks to the Corinthians because of their routine of saying yes to their desires. They had a saying that "food is for the stomach" and believed that if I became hungry, then I should go eat. The same way they felt about that desire they felt towards sex. If I become horny, then clearly, I need to indulge in sex rather or not I am married. As a generation (myself included), we live by this slogan without saying it. We've gone so deep into the sin that we don't even recognize it as sin. But one day, God will bring it to light, and when He does, we will suffer from what we thought was good. I have experience in that.

I didn't go with my head held high when I left the trap. I ran in shame to a dark place. Depression! It was in this place that I felt that I was losing. It was there where the thoughts were winning. They had authority over me. Withholding control over me, I let them win. If I were going through a depressing day, I would sit in my room most of the day and try to sleep it off. But if I had to work or go to class on those days I was depressed, I would go through the motions of life—no smile on my face. I was thinking about how I couldn't wait to be alone. Praying was hard on that day. I would get in God's presence and say, "I don't know what's wrong with me." I lacked words to speak to the one who could change it all. I let shame hold me back from going into His presence. I just felt too much like a failure to go into His presence. I mean, half of the time, I purposely went to temptation. But the great news is that He hears our hearts, and we have an Advocate, the Holy Spirit, who steps in and prays for us when we don't know what to pray for *(Romans 8:26)*.

As I admitted at the beginning of this book, depression prolonged my writing. It was hard those days when my depression was running rapidly to try to do anything. Rather than typing up a chapter or doing schoolwork, I procrastinated habitually. I would justify it by telling myself I would get around to it once I "felt" like it. Because of my thoughts, I wasn't mentally ready to do anything. I'll get a little more into my depression in the next chapter, but it stopped me from walking on purpose. It even got worse, but I'll get into that later.

It was hard to get out of that place. I believed that there was no way that God would still use me, and at a time, I even agreed there was no way God still loved me. Then I had to remember that God doesn't just throw the towel in on people like that. I realized it had to be the enemy trying to convince me of that. Here's something about the enemy: HE IS A LAIR. I mean, my mistakes were terrible, and my mistakes; well, let me stop saying mistakes and use sin. My sins made me feel unholy. But at the end of the day, he is a liar, and what he tries to do daily is feed us lies that will make us give up and run from the blessings and the love that God has for us. And that's precisely what I did. I started to run! I felt ashamed of the things that I had done. Like how could you be like this? How can you want to be somebody who stands up and preaches God's Word, but then on Saturday night, you're out drinking and whatnot, or there is a different girl over every other week? How can you call yourself a follower of Christ?

Those were the kind of thoughts that ran through my mind. And it had gotten so bad that I came to that point where I just figured that God didn't love me. I had no problem telling somebody else that God loves you despite your mistake, sin, or past. Yet, I couldn't comprehend that God would love somebody like me anymore. Not me, nope, not at all. You may be feeling like me. You might be trapped in your head and feel there is no escape. That sucks, and I know the feeling because I felt that way for months. I felt God was tallying every sin I had committed and shaking His head in disgust. I mean, who wouldn't? I felt as if I deserved all the yelling. That's what I was used to when I made mistakes anyway. Growing up, I got yelled at way more than I heard the word congratulations! There was my problem.

I was viewing God based on how humans treated me. The worst thing you can ever do is put God into the same box that the world treats you. Viewing God the same way that others treat you is just a self-defeating tool. It's a trick from the enemy that can tear you apart. The reality is God is nothing like how the world treats you. This world may treat us in a way that breaks us down and hurts us, but God doesn't. He is patient and kind, knowing that we will struggle and fall, but His love is faithful and drives away all lies.

It's beautiful that Christ meets us in our weakness and frees us from condemnation *(Romans 8:1)*. The enemy doesn't want you to know that. He would love for you never to let go because if you get freedom, he loses, and he knows you will go and help somebody else. There is grace for us. There is mercy. God wants to free us from our past. He doesn't want anybody to perish but is so patient that He is waiting for us to repent *(2 Peter 3:9)*. You can find this grace and mercy in Christ our Lord.

John 1:14, "And the Word became flesh and dwelt among us, and we beheld His glory, the glory as of the only begotten of the Father, full of grace and truth."

Full of grace and truth is what our savior is. Grace is God's lovingkindness divine favor that gives joy and is a gift. We didn't do anything to deserve His grace, yet He still gave it to us. His grace covers us in our mistakes. When I found myself dealing with my mistakes, His grace reminded me that I still had favor in His sight. You may wonder what you can do to get His grace. There is nothing you can do. It's free. My mistakes made me feel as if I was chained up, but His grace set me free. Ephesians 2: 8-9 says, "Forby grace you have been saved through faith, and that not of yourselves; it is the gift of God, not of works, lest anyone should boast." Grace is what saves us, but to be saved and set free, we need to have faith. Faith is not the cause for grace but the connection to grace. To get the gift of grace, we must believe that grace has saved us and set us free. I have to have faith to believe that. Without faith, it is impossible to see yourself as free.

Truth is the revelation of things. Christ would reveal to us the truth about supernatural things and natural things. He was fully man and fully God, so He has authority over the flesh. When I think about being full of grace and truth, I see a parent who sees his child in a moment where they have made a mistake, and he shows love to that child. But he also corrects that child and shows them the way to which is correct. That is how God is with us. He uses our mistakes and doesn't tally up looking to condemn us but a moment to teach us a lesson that helps us grow.

God never created us to struggle all through life. I learned through His grace that I was not my past nor my past control my now or future. So, brothers and sisters, it's time to fight against the subconscious mind. You have to empty every last single thing that is holding you back. It might not be something you want to do, but it is essential for yourself, your future, and everything connected to you that you go through this process. You are designed in such a way that not only will you get through the fight but will indeed thrive in the middle of the fight. The voices may never go away in your mind, but don't let the voices win; prove the voices wrong. It's you vs you! And you are not your thoughts.

"You are designed in such a way that not only will you get through the fight but will indeed thrive in the middle of the fight."

QUESTIONS TO ASK SELF

1. What are the voices in your mind telling you about yourself? If there are any lies, what scriptures do you think will cast down those lies?

2. What do you focus on more? The negatives or the positives? How do you think you can focus more on the positives in your life?

3. In what ways have you unconsciously viewed God because of how people have treated you?

4. The fight is all about you vs you. In what ways have you self-sabotaged yourself? How do you plan on overcoming the mistakes that you made?

I JUST WANT TO BE NORMAL

"God didn't create me to be normal. He didn't create me to fit in. He created me to stand out and lead. I must accept not being normal."

- **Tavonne Bowman**

I knew going to college wouldn't be a walk in the park. I wasn't going to be able to smile my way through this. I knew that it was going to be a challenge for me. What I love about myself, though, is that I love challenges. I love adversity. I love the idea of having my back against the wall and all odds stacked against me. It's something about those moments that I absolutely love. The motivation kicks into overdrive. I get pumped up, and I tell myself we can do this. Well, those exact moments I loved were the ones I absolutely hated.

I was stressed out! School was kicking me, money was punching me, relationships were slamming me on my neck, and my purpose for living seemed like it was fading away. I couldn't take it anymore. It all started during my junior year of college, in the fall of 2019. Before this time, life was exemplary. I had no problems. All I had to do was school, work, and sports. But it became my turn to go through life.

It was interesting timing for this storm coming my way. I had just started my campus ministry, leading a bible study called "I AM bible study." I don't know why I thought I was so untouchable because I was doing God's work. Life was like, "lol, that's cute, but here are some identity problems. And while we are at it, let me throw in these relationship issues. A couple of deaths close to you, add on having a couple of classes that you are failing right now and jobs saying no to you, so that means no money". That's actually when the fight becomes harder.

I was living out the phrase, "If it's not one thing, it's another." In less than 24 hours, I had a friend and grandfather die. People were telling me that I was doing a great job leading bible study and that it was impactful, but on the inside, I thought the opposite. I questioned if God had even wanted me to do this. I was surprised to learn I was making an impact like I wanted to due to this feeling. Then, I had two classes (I can't remember what they were) stressing me out. Every college student knows that you always have that one class every semester, that by the end of it, you shrug your shoulders and say whatever grade I get, I get.

I was really at my breaking point, man. It was awful. Yet, like any adversity I faced, I took a step back, analyzed the issue, and asked myself what I must do to get out of this. I remember hearing somebody talk about counseling and how we should partake in it because it would be healthy. So, I decided to seek it out, and it was just my blessing that my university offered it for all students.

My first meeting was in a group setting, and I was not too fond of it. This girl's anxiety was making me worse. She shook her leg the whole meeting to the point where I just got up and left. When I had my first individual meeting, my counselor asked me about it, and I told her I didn't want a group meeting. Individual sessions allowed me to be free, and let me say I was free in the first meeting. I started crying and did not stop for 5 minutes. I can't remember what we talked about, but I know I released a lot of stuff I needed to release.

Therapy became a part of my college life routine. Every other Wednesday during my junior through senior year, I walked from my apartment through the Akron campus, heading to Simmons Hall. Walking to Simmons Hall, I wondered what I would say to my counselor today. Even though my counselor reminded me so much of my grandmother, whom I could comfortably talk to about anything yet, I was still nervous. Some days, I walk into the room with so much to pour out, then other days, I stare at the clock in front of me, waiting for the hour to be over because I have nothing to say. On those days, going to therapy felt so pointless to me. I thought it was a waste of time because I wasn't gaining anything. I was just there because I scheduled the meeting and wanted to check it off my weekly list. I would still feel the same way I felt before I came, so what was the point of all this?

That's what I hated most about my depression. The mood swings that I was experiencing. It felt so much like a roller coaster ride. There are days when I feel like me. Energetic, smiling, happy, ready to conquer life, and passionately looking for somebody to inspire. Then, there are days when I feel stuck, defeated, useless, and forgotten. I fought this mood for three years. Nobody knew that when I was at parties getting drunk, I was using drinking to fight my depression. It was something about drinking that made me feel good again. It made me feel like the me that I would be if I weren't fighting depression—the life of the party or the person who makes everybody laugh. I didn't think that I could be that same me, though, when I was down. I was too busy stuck in my mind, so I turned to drinking to get out of my mind. If I heard we were drinking tonight, I would be somewhere in the background saying bet, let's go. I knew I would drink past my limits, but I didn't care because I wanted to forget my issues.

It got worse during the pandemic. We can all agree that it was awful at the heart of the pandemic. Just sitting in the house all day with nothing to do sucked. Going to school online made me miss being able to go to class in person (even if I would like to daydream in class). It just was so frustrating. The last straw for me was the church going from in-person to online. If you go to church, you know how different the feeling is watching it online. It is not the same! I have to be honest about that. I found myself learning to create my worship, but even that was hard. On the days when I couldn't carry myself into prayer, I needed somebody to help me, and the fellowship of others helped. But during the pandemic, I had nobody. The church was where I didn't need to ask somebody to help me worship, but hearing the shouts and cries carried me to God's throne room. Even with the pandemic being a struggle, I needed it. The pandemic removed a lot of baggage for me.

One day after bible study, one of those bags was opened. The room cleared out, leaving just me and a couple of friends with whom I knew I could have a vulnerable moment. It's very healthy and necessary to have a circle of people with whom you can be vulnerable. You need people you can turn to when you are weak. We were not created to be isolated or emotionless people. God created humans for each other. If the circle of people you hang around is not the people you can be weak around, then it's time for you to change the people you hang out with.

I am thankful for the friends I met in college who turned into family. I am not knocking the friends I grew up with, but if you went to college, you understand the bond you create with others in college with you. I can gratefully say that I have friends both before and while in college that I cherish. However, the friends I met in college (I actually met Tony when we were 13, but we both went to college together) walked with me through the stressful valley that college brought. We built a bond together. We watch each other grow up from young adult to adult. We cried, laughed, and argued together. We became each other's accountability partners and prayer partners. And the support for each other was always there. No matter the goal one of the friends had, everybody showed up and supported each other because everybody wanted to see each other win.

When it came to my bible study, these friends made sure to be there. They would give me some pointers on how they felt bible study went. Sometimes, they would tell me to do something differently next week, and other times, they would tell me how good the message was. On this day, I was about to have one of my most vulnerable moments with my friends. As we (Tony, Ray, Aloni, Kylah, and I) were getting ready to leave, Kylah looked at me with a smile and said, "That was a great discussion." With my head down, trying to fight back tears, I sighed and said, "I don't think I did well today." Yes, everybody was really into the conversation, but I don't think I got them to understand my point. Right, there was my breaking point. I couldn't hold back the tears, so I let them out. As they came running down my cheeks, everything I felt in my heart went out of my mouth. "I feel like I am failing at this, y'all. I don't think I'm making the impact I want to make." At this point, Kylah saw that I was letting negative thoughts win. She stopped me from talking and reminded me that I was reaching people who hadn't attended the other bible studies on campus before I started mine. After her, the rest of my friends encouraged me and reminded me that my passion for Christ also helps them pursue their desire for Him.

As much of an encouraging moment that was, it still wasn't enough with everything else going on. I felt like the only way to stop this painful, crushing weight was to die. Times that I cried, I would talk to God, telling Him how I just wanted to come home. That's how bad it got for me. I wanted out of this world. I would think about hanging or stabbing myself, but I never went through with the thought. I never even attempted it. But it didn't stop me from thinking about it. I was tired of fighting all the voices in my mind. I was tired of the mistakes that I made. I was tired of feeling stuck. I didn't feel like I was enough. I was empty on the inside and just wanted out. I didn't want to face another fight. I was exhausted. That seemed like the perfect, straightforward plan. Die, and guess what? You don't have to suffer anymore. You can go live at peace with God in heaven.

But instead of doing it, the Holy Spirit would give me visions of what it would be like if I left. I would lay there and envision my funeral. I think it was good that I had these visions because each time I would think about how life would be best without me in it, God would show me hearts that would be broken if I wasn't here. I saw my mother crying, my little brother confused, and a cousin broken into pieces. That vision helped me not kill myself. All I could do when the idea came around was cry. The weight I was feeling was hard, but I knew I couldn't give up on the people who loved me, and I couldn't give up on God. I was glad that God stopped me and never answered that prayer. Instead, He showed me something important! And used my therapist to speak life into me.

Different is what I was meant to be

As usual, I came to the same building, marched up the stairs to my counselor's office, and waited for her to meet me. She always met me with a smile, which made me feel more comfortable. As we walked into her office, I knew that today was the day I would try to cruise through the meeting. Usually, when I go in, I sit in a chair and grab the pillow next to me, but this time, I sat on the floor next to the chair and didn't say anything. She looked at me and asked what's wrong? I knew what I wanted to say, but I just put my head down and looked at the floor. The silence continued for a minute, and then I said, "I just want to be normal."

As I said this, tears began to run down my face. She waited a couple more minutes before opening her mouth to ask, "What do you mean?". I sat and thought about what I meant, then explained myself. "I don't feel normal. I feel like I'm strange for being depressed. I'm tired of feeling like this. I'm tired of going through these moods where I know I can conquer the world one day, and the next day, I want to give up. I'm tired of fighting this. I'm tired of waking up happy one day, then the next day, I don't even want to get out of bed. I want to be normal". I was tired of hearing those voices in my head screaming at me. I was even tired of being tired. I was over that achy pain that pierced my heart. It made me feel empty on the inside. My soul is screaming for help while my mind is trying to find the answers to how we come out of this.

Being around people didn't immensely help this emotional rollercoaster I was on. Whenever I was around people, I thought, why can't I be happy like them? Here I am, faking my smiles, knowing I felt empty inside while their smiles and laughter felt authentic. Then, a revelation came to me. What if you are not the only one struggling with this? What if, just like you, somebody here is smiling through the pain now but crying later? I didn't stop to think about how they were in private. I had no way of knowing if something was bothering them, but I sure looked at them, then looked at me and said why are we so crippled in our mind. But the reality was I had to realize that I was not alone in this fight.

As the silence continued, with more tears rolling down my face, she said, "Just because you are fighting something doesn't make you weird or anything. You weren't created to be normal; God created you to be different. To be set apart." She always helped me incorporate my faith into my issues. I had to let that sink in. As I sat and thought about it, she was right. I was created differently, and this condition that I was fighting was not who I was but just a trial that I had to go through to be able to minister to people in this same area. Almost every victorious person we have read in the Bible about or seen personally had a struggle. For victory to occur, there must be an obstacle to go through. This was my battle to fight. To win the war against depression and show somebody else how they can also overcome it. So, just because I was going through a storm. I had to remind myself that just because we are going through something doesn't mean we are "different" in a negative way. It means that we are human, and this is just our season to go through something. Does it make the issue better? No. But it provides a new perspective. What I go through does not define who I am! It just tells a story of what I have been through.

What are you facing? How does it make you feel? Are you tired of facing this same battle? Are you ready to quit? I understand that you may be exhausted, but after this battle, there will be a story to tell. You will have a testimony of how God brought you through. And that testimony will be used as a weapon for somebody else to overcome the same problem you are facing!

Empty No More

For a person who has never dealt with feeling empty on the inside, that description can confuse you. How can one feel empty? What does that mean? Emptiness is a paralyzed emotional state. It's like getting punched in the face but feeling no pain. When I should have been happy, I showed no expression. When asked if everything was okay with me, I usually couldn't give an accurate answer. The emptiness left me without words to describe the pain I was feeling. I just knew I had a burden on me that I was tired of carrying.

I knew that I was missing something. My first thought wasn't, "You're missing that relationship with God," because I was going to church, praying, worshipping, and reading my Bible. Then, I thought it was relationships. I thought I would be fine if I could get into one of those. I was wrong there. Every "talking" stage I walked into, I left more drained than before. It may be the job, then. I was wrong again. Yes, I have had jobs that stressed me out, but now that I have a more peaceful job, it wasn't that.

Was it friends? No! Was it my family? No! So, I had to face the fact that it was my relationship with God. Reality had to sit in for me. Even though I grew up in the church and hated missing a Sunday service, my relationship with God was suffering. And it wasn't because of God. It was me. I had neglected a deep, intimate relationship with God. Instead of running to Him when I felt empty, I would run to anything but Him! I ran to places like sex, drinking, and partying. I was told doing these things would make me feel better, but I felt worse. I felt ashamed. I had abandoned God when He was the only one that could fill me up.

I treated my relationship with Him like it meant nothing to me. Yes, I would pray and read my Bible, but I was going through the motions. It was like I was doing it just to do it. Many Christians probably won't admit it or are unaware that sometimes our relationship with God can go on autopilot. We get so caught up in our everyday lives that we don't take the time to go deeper with God but scratch the surface daily. The good thing to note is that even though we are on autopilot, God is not. He will do what is necessary to get us off autopilot and into deeper worship with Him. But doing this means He has to shake up our foundations to grab our attention. Mentally, I was shaken up, but I'm thankful for Romans 8:28! It was for my good that I had that shake-up because it drew me to go back to God.

The prodigal son had his foundation shaken. It all started when the son wanted to be greedy and impatient with an inheritance he was not ready for. At his request, the father gave him his share of the estate. This young boy went off into a distant country only to blow all he had and found himself eating with pigs. This boy went from living in a palace to a pigsty, all because of his temporary desire. When he realized that his wants led him to emptiness, he realized that only his father could supply what he truly needed.

Where have your desires led you? Places that you were never supposed to be? With crowds, you were never supposed to come in connection with? A connection that could have been avoided if you had just stayed put. I wasn't empty before I followed my wants over my needs. I felt just fine before I dined with those I shouldn't have. But here I was, now realizing that only God could satisfy me. So, how do I get back to "normal"?

Embracing the Difference

As that meeting closed, I got off the floor, wiped the tears off my face, and scheduled myself for our next meeting next week. She walked me to the front desk and said, "See you next week," with a smile. Walking out the door, I inserted my headphones and turned to my gospel playlist. Just like I would walk to Simmons thinking about what I would say, I walked home debriefing everything. What stood out most was "you were meant to be different." I grew up with the mindset to always be set apart. Separate yourself from the crowd because fitting in will get you nowhere. So, why was I saying I want to be normal now? Why did I think that my issue was my identity? Why did I believe that I could never overcome what I battled within?

"Just because you are fighting something doesn't make you weird or anything. You weren't created to be normal; you were created to be different".

I had to embrace the idea that I was different. When God created humans, He took His time and made each of us uniquely. Even twins that look alike are still distinct. We each have different fingerprints. Different lifestyle. Different voice. Different identities. Giving into peer pressure and worldly cultures is what takes away from our uniqueness.

Even the trials we face make us who we are. That's why we must learn to embrace the difference. It helps us to stand out. It makes you, you! So, embrace the fight. Embrace the trials and tribulations. Count it all joy because God has placed you in that battle because He believes in you. There is a phrase that says, "God gives His strongest battles to His strongest soldiers." I think the saying should go, "God gives His toughest battles to those who will trust in His strength." Take Job for an example. He was chilling, minding his business, but the devil and God made a bet one day. The devil came into the presence of God, and God asked him what he was doing there. He goes on to tell the Lord why he was there, and God says, ***"Have you considered My Servant Job, that there is none like him on the earth, a blameless and upright man, one who fears God and shuns evil?" (Job 1:8).*** God gave Job this prestige recognition. But Satan believed Job was only this way because God had protected him, and if he stopped protecting him, he would curse God. Well, God permitted Satan to come up against everything but Job's life. Job lost everything! To the point of facing death thinking this was it. Job did have one fear, which was losing everything. He admits this fear, stating, "What I have feared the most has come up against m1e" (Job 3:25). Job was not a poor man. He was rich, and just like that, it was all gone. I know this story sounds crazy, like why would God allow this?

The truth is that He allowed this because He knew Job was built differently. I mean, He said it Himself. He calls Job a man who fears God. The meaning of fearing God is to show respect to him. He knew that Job was going to respect Him no matter what. He knew that Job wasn't going to turn his back on God. What Job went through would soon be used as a testimony for others around him.

Your struggle, fight, or depression does not own you, but you own it! I need you to declare this. I am built differently. I am made for this. God placed you in this trial, battle, and storm because He knew that you would overcome this. He knew you would have a testimony after all the hell you have been through. He knew that no matter how hard it got or how many times you said you would quit, you wouldn't give up.

So, listen to me! I know this sucks. I know you hate feeling like this. Trust me; I do, too. But we are built differently. We don't quit. What we do is get creative and figure out how we overcome this. Think about the other times you felt like quitting. What did you do? You might have taken some days and just sat with it, and that's cool. But you also decided to say I won't allow this to have control over me. You prayed, found wisdom, and changed how you did things because you were tired of the struggle.

You're probably shaking your head and laughing like, "he is right." I know I am because it's the truth. You and I are warriors; we don't allow anything to weigh us down for too long. It's only a matter of time until we start to swing back, and today is that day because we are built differently! Hold on to this one truth. God is in three places. At the start, telling you to start. In the middle of it with and encouraging you. And at the finish line, waiting for you to get there because He has faith you will make it there! Keep pushing forward!

QUESTIONS TO ASK SELF

1. If you struggle with depression and keep things bottled up, why are you reluctant to seek help? What are some positives you think you can gain from counseling?

2. What broken area have you been in? What testimony do you have from that area? How do you think God wants to use you in that area to minister to others? (You should spend time praying to God about this question.)

3. How can you start owning your brokenness? What can you do to remind yourself daily that you are not what you go through?

4. What is something in your life you wish were different but need to start embracing?

MOVING FORWARD

"The truth is unless you let go, unless you forgive yourself, unless you forgive the situation unless you realize that the situation is over, you cannot move forward."

- Steve Maraboli

"No, dear brothers and sisters, I have not achieved it, but I focus on this one thing: Forgetting the past and looking forward to what lies ahead, I press on to reach the end of the race and receive the heavenly prize for which God, through Christ Jesus, is calling us."

- Philippians 3 v 13-14

After listening to me ramble on about a particular situation-ship, my counselor suggested that I was dealing with an ambiguous loss in one of our sessions. I didn't know what this phrase meant, so I looked it up. An ambiguous loss is a loss that occurs, yet it leaves you without a clear understanding or closure as to why. It is usually used when somebody has lost a loved one, yet they're searching for answers to why this happened, delaying their grief. It made sense that she would describe my situation because I was searching for an answer to why this person and I never worked. I was delaying my grief, and I certainly had not let go. I was living in my past while my body was in my present, and man, it sucks.

Talking about this makes me feel so embarrassed. Since I was holding on to this unanswered question, it made it hard for me to move on with my life. I put my life on hold for somebody I knew deep down inside wasn't coming back. I fought internally between walking away and waiting in hope (I wish I would have walked away.) But while part of me screamed whenever she came across my mind telling me to give it up, I listened to the side that wanted to wait in hope. I hated that for myself, however. It was the wrong side to listen to because I played my past repeatedly over in my mind, trying to think of ways I could have done something different so that I wouldn't be battling this.

It really didn't matter what I replayed, however. What was done was done, and it couldn't change it. I just needed to let go but couldn't, all because I wanted my question of why to be answered. People who deal with an "ambiguous loss" tend to go down a road of unforgiveness. We will replay everything in our minds, find every mistake we made, and then blame ourselves for them leaving. We don't wonder if it wasn't meant to be or if they were going through their stuff. No, we sit there and blame ourselves for why things are not different. You would think that accepting what is gone would be easy, but when you have so much faith and hope, it's hard to do. When you pray to God to make it work, even though you heard God say this is the one, it's not as easy. It is never easy to move on from something that you prayed for.

Accept what is lost

Steve Maraboli stated, ***"The truth is unless you let go, unless you forgive yourself, unless you forgive the situation, unless you realize that the situation is over, you cannot move forward."*** He states four moves that must be made before a person can move forward. Let go, forgive yourself, forgive the situation, and realize it's over. Three of those steps have been the most intricate steps to climb. I didn't forgive myself or the situation. I hadn't let go and realized that the problem was over. Instead, I sat with a lustful hope (not Godly), thinking that there was at least some flame still burning. I knew the situation was dead and gone, yet I couldn't be honest with myself.

Everybody around me, even my counselor, didn't understand why I held on. They all told me it was time to move on, but I ignored their voices and chose to wait. I thought that I was doing God's will by waiting, but what I was doing was causing me delayed pain that turned into present suffering. I had to ask myself why I was still holding on. Why is it hard for me to forgive myself for that day? Why can't I realize that the situation is over? I don't know what I tell myself some days. I think I have forgiven myself and moved on. Still, I find myself replaying the moment, asking myself, "How could you be that immature, Tavonne?". As that moment plays back and forth, it's that moment that stops me from focusing on my now. When will I be honest with myself and let myself know that what is done is done? We can't change the past, but we can make sure our future isn't a past cycle!

The only way to answer the question of why accurately is by first stating that I try to be a perfectionist in all I do. This is the worst thing you can try to be because nobody is perfect. But being a perfectionist is something I couldn't break. In high school, I wanted to be perfect on the field or court so my coaches could applaud me. I looked perfect with my mother or grandparents so they could see I wasn't like my father. I even tried to be perfect for God. Guess what? I failed at it. I made mistakes on the football field, like getting suspended and benched while being a team captain. I even heard the words "just like his father was" spelled out of my grandmother's. That broke my soul. And to add on the number of times I have sinned against God! Those moments left me ashamed and pushed me into depression and self-hate.

Am I my mistakes? No! Do my flaws represent my character? No! Yet, you could see me sitting in a prison cell with the gates open for me to leave, but I don't even move. Instead of walking out the door of a house on fire, I chose to stay breathing in the toxic chemicals. I had freedom knocking on my door, but I didn't answer. All because of the childish mistakes that I made as a child! I beat myself up for doing immature and idiotic stuff while forgetting that I was young, and these are the ages when we make silly mistakes.

Moses is an excellent example of somebody who didn't forgive themselves or the situation. This is also one of my favorite stories because I relate to it. In Exodus 3, Moses was tendering to his father-in-law's sheep when God appeared to him in a burning bush, speaking to him about the children of Israel being enslaved.

Exodus 3: 6-8, 10-12 "6 And He said, "I am the God of your father—the God of Abraham, the God of Isaac, and the God of Jacob." Then

Moses hid his face, for he was afraid to look at God. 7 And the Lord said, "I have surely seen the oppression of My people who are in Egypt, and have heard their outcry because of their taskmasters, for I am aware of their sufferings. 8 So I have come down to rescue them from the power of the Egyptians, and to bring them up from that land to a good and spacious land, to a land flowing with milk and honey, to the place of the Canaanite, the Hittite, the Amorite, the Perizzite, the Hivite, and the Jebusite....

10 And now come, and I will send you to Pharaoh, so that you may bring My people, the sons of Israel, out of Egypt." 11 But Moses said to God, "Who am I, that I should go to Pharaoh, and that I should bring the sons of Israel out of Egypt?" 12 And He said, "Assuredly I will be with you, and this shall be the sign to you that it is I who have sent you: when you have brought the people out of Egypt, you shall worship God at this mountain."

God calls on Moses to free the people of Israel and lead them to victory. Instead of going, Moses questions his ability to lead. The almighty God, who will never put us in a position to fail, called for Moses, but he should be there doubting. To understand this story, you must read the previous chapter and know the history. In chapter 2, Moses was born. For the first 40 years of his life, he walked under the impression that he was called to lead the children of Israel from bondage, but one mistake one day shattered his confidence. One day, an Egyptian and a Hebrew were fighting, so Moses intervened on the Hebrew's behalf, killing the Egyptians. The next day, though, seeing two Hebrews fight, Moses only breaks up the fight and asks why the brothers are fighting. One of the Hebrews responds by mentioning what Moses did the other day. "***14 But he said, "Who made you a ruler and a judge over us? Do you [r]intend to kill me as you killed the Egyptian?" Then Moses was afraid and said, "Surely the matter has become known!" (Exodus 2:14).*** Moses then relives that mistake for the next 40 years in his mind, causing him to doubt when God called him to lead.

No more looking back

How do you feel after you've committed a mistake? Do you think about it for a minute and then move on, or do you allow that one issue to hinder you in the future? Moses's mistake took him down a path of low self-esteem. He couldn't see that God (who is omnipresent) knows our past, present, and future and was calling on him to do great works. God did not care about the mistake that he had previously made. God was showing that He is the God of a second chance. He is not like a man. Man will cancel you because of your mistakes, yet God will show you how to do it correctly. Your mistakes do not define you; God uses them to refine you. One of my favorite verses is Philippians 3:13-14. Paul is the author of this book, and if you read Paul's letters, he sometimes compares the Christian life to an Olympic race. In these two verses, we see an example of it. ***"No, dear brothers and sisters, I have not achieved it, but I focus on this one thing: Forgetting the past and looking forward to what lies ahead, I press on to reach the end of the race and receive the heavenly prize for which God, through Christ Jesus, is calling us" (Philippians 3 v 13-14)***.

I ran track in high school. Since we didn't have a lot of track players sometimes, I would have to run long-distance races. In this one long-distance race, I started leading the first four laps, then after leading four straight laps, I found myself dead last and finally getting overlapped. What happened? I grew tired, but most importantly, I looked back. And the more I looked back to see what was behind me, the more I lost the lead. I was worrying so much about getting passed up that I couldn't focus on returning to the top where I once was leading four laps. Coaches tell their runners to avoid looking back into somebody else's lane. It's that split second where you look behind or to the side of you, and you lose focus and get slowed down by worrying.

It's the same with life. Every mistake, every sin, every time I choose wrong over right, I look back and ponder those moments. I prefer to allow those moments to live rent-free in my head day in and day out. Instead of looking forward, I continued to look behind me. This has been slowing me down for too long. Some days, I crash out because of my inability to focus forward. Sometimes, I sit in depression or have low self-esteem due to it. I walk with this weight on my shoulder, not understanding Jesus had already destroyed the weight of my past. I needed to let go, but I just couldn't. I had to live in my past and walk into my now. But how?

No more living in regret

In this encounter with God, Moses didn't have an unbelief problem that God couldn't do it. He had an unbelief problem that he couldn't do. He had given up all hope in the very purpose he was called to. He looked into the mirror and saw what everybody else around him saw. He was a dude who lacked self-control and didn't know one thing about leading. This left him asking God one question. "Who am I that I should go?". It's a great question, depending on how you view it. I can say that Moses is asking God to show him his identity, but Moses is showing us his inability to believe.

God was calling Moses into purpose, yet he lived in his past. He could not see that God was calling him by what God had purposed for him and not by what he had done. A man brought up Moses's past while God called him into his future. Yet because of the rejection of his people, Moses imprisoned himself in regret. For 40 years, Moses paced back and forth in his mind, replaying that moment of his life. He probably questioned himself about what he could have done differently to avoid this. But there was nothing left for him to do.

Do you replay certain events over and over in your mind? It's okay to admit that you do. We all do. We think about how we could have said something differently, done something differently, or even removed ourselves from a situation sooner rather than later.

There is nothing wrong with relooking at the past. But what do you get out of looking back on the past? How does it leave you feeling? Nothing good can come from taking yourself back to the place where

"Your mistakes do not define you; God uses them to refine you."

you felt most like a failure. All you are doing is killing your self-confidence in yourself. You are slowing yourself down, and it's time that you stop. Why? Because you need to be your best friend and not your worst enemy. You need to believe in yourself to walk on purpose. Your inability to believe hinders you from walking in your God-given purpose.

So, the past you are currently replaying in your mind. Do this huge favor for me and tell your history, "I can no longer live here." You must get up and leave the prison doors God has opened for you.

God can forgive you, but until you forgive yourself, there is no true peace of mind. Until you process the fact that God has given you forgiveness, it's hard for you to comprehend forgiveness for yourself. The truth is God doesn't hold our sins against us. ***"If we confess our sins, he is faithful and just to forgive us our sins and to cleanse us from all unrighteousness" (1 John 1:9).*** It's the "if" that is important. You have to make the honest confession, "Yes, I've sinned and fallen short of your glory," but God, I need you. Then grab hold of the truth that he is faithful and cleanse us. When we wrap that around our heads, we can genuinely receive forgiveness.

Give yourself grace

This is an essential step to moving forward: Give yourself grace. This means letting go of the idea that everybody has to be perfect. In this place, you can mess up and not think it's the end of the world. It's where you have the right to feel overwhelmed. You realize you do not have to hit it out of the park. You know it's best to take it "one day at a time."

If I were you, I would highlight that quote. One day at a time! My good sister Ari mentioned that to me one day, and it has forever stuck with me. That phrase helped me remind myself that we don't have to rush to the finish line. There is a certain pace that one's life is supposed to be like, and it's at that pace one must go. Taking it one day at a time means not living in my past or future but walking in my now! I let go of all things I cannot control and allow God to be God. I finish the plate before me and do not think about the next meal. Taking it one day at a time removes all worry and anxiety. It also teaches you how to love yourself. And loving you is vital to your future.

Loving you has to be vital to moving forward. Loving you does not mean being selfish to the rest of the world. Loving yourself moves regret out and brings grace in. It's discerning where and where not to give your time—knowing who and who not to allow into your life. It is setting the necessary boundaries that need to be placed. Also, it is about allowing yourself to relapse or fall, then picking yourself back up and saying, "Okay, that's fine. We made a mistake now; how can I not make this same mistake again?".

Heal before going forward.

Before we go to the last chapter, I want to drop one more thing on you. Before you move forward to whatever is next. Whether it's a new job, relationship, church, or friendship, whatever has caused you to hurt, before you go to the next place, you need to heal first. I had to learn it the hard way. I was trying to move on with my life and meet new people, yet I had not let go of the last person. I was dating new people while still married to the past. And every time I told myself that we had healed, it took one conversation with a friend to realize I didn't. I was saying, "I'm healed," then turning around and saying, "I can't trust nobody." I was proclaiming to be free while telling people I have reasons for not allowing people close to me. It's all because I faked my healing.

Faking healing is something that people often do intentionally and sometimes without knowing. People who do it deliberately are the ones who want to ignore the pain, avoid help, and fill a void with temporary things. We've all done this before. Nights when we were hurting, we called over the same person that hurt us or connected with somebody that we knew we shouldn't have. We talked to people that didn't fit us. Or we meet the right person in the wrong season of our lives, but because we ignored the hurt, we bleed out on them, destroying what could have been. Then, the people who do it without knowing will soon realize they are hurting at the wrong time. These types of people go from person to person and place to place with nothing working, left wondering why it's not working. This feeling leaves them facing the mirror with tears streaming down their faces, saying, "It was me the whole time." I've been both of these types of people. I spent one year ignoring my pain and just doing anything, not knowing that I was doing all the stuff that I would not do if I were whole. I would not have slid into the DMs of a lot of girls, let half of them over, or even have sex with them if I wasn't trying to fill a void. Then I went another year thinking I was healed from the pain, not knowing that there was still more to the process. It was weird to me because I wasn't feeling the pain, but when I would talk to somebody, I couldn't open up. I didn't have it in me to open up. I grew nervous when I heard a girl say she liked me. My heart says not again when an ounce of feelings starts to flow through my bones. I was traumatized but paralyzed by the emotions. I asked God why I couldn't connect, open up, and be with somebody. I faced myself man to man and asked, "Are we really healed?"

Jesus in John 5 runs into this man at the pool of Bethesda and asks Him the same type of question. At this pool, all kinds of people required healing. Sick, blind, lame, and paralyzed were all here waiting for an angel to come at a particular time to stir up the pool. The first person to step into the pool would be the one to be healed. This man was there for THIRTY-EIGHT YEARS! That's insane. For 38 years, this man could not develop some strategy to get himself in the water. For 38 years, this man has found himself in last place. For 38 years, he was stuck. People were coming and going, being healed, yet this man was still broken. Jesus stepped on the scene and saw this man. He asks the most straightforward yet powerful question, "Do you want to be made well?". The man responded with excuses. He blamed being stuck in the same place not on himself but on everybody around him. he said nobody helped him or people jumped in front of him. But what he should have been talking about is himself. Why was it that for 38 years, he didn't think of a way? No ideas, no strategies. We, too, become this man. Complacent with being broken. Excuses for not being healed.

Who do you blame for your hurt? Are you still blaming that person for hurting you? Seriously!? It's been two years. That happened 4 Christmases ago, and you still haven't contacted your family? That relationship was three years ago! Don't say you're stuck either because you're not. You are living in your pain. There is a vast difference between being stuck and living. Stuck is when something is preventing you from moving. Living is when you have gotten comfortable being in that place or settled there. So, stop with the "Oh, I'm stuck here"; no, you're comfortable living here! You'll love it there. You see no reason to move on. You are asking yourself why would we ever move on when holding on to the pain is so much easier. But what if I told you that what's more accessible is not always necessary? And easier is not always probable. The hurt has consumed you so much that you can't see that healing is waiting for you to let go!

So let go. It's time to let go and move on. There is no point in living here no more. There is nothing that you can do to change what happened. There's no time-traveling mission for you where you can go back and avoid what happened. What happened needed to happen for a reason. It was for your good. Does it suck that it happened? Absolutely! But it is not the end.

I realized I had difficulty letting go because I didn't want to be wrong. I didn't want to deal with the shame that somebody I believed would be forever would no longer be here. I labeled it as God was in it when God wasn't there anymore. I misinterpreted what He said. I did not want to agree that it was time to let go. But the truth was the season was changing, and it was time to move on. I also had to understand there is no shame in hearing God wrong or wanting to hold on. Many people have thought they heard God say something, and He said something else. You won't always hear Him right, and that's okay. You are not always going to want to let go. Especially when you felt that this was a promise from God. But I learned that even with the promises He gives us. It is okay to give them back to him. Maybe He wants the promise back to develop you more before He returns the promise to you. Surrendering back to God is a great move to make. It is the first step to stop living in pain and start walking in victory!

Don't let shame hold you back from your healing. There's nothing to be ashamed of because we all have experienced hurt. Some hurt is worse than others, but we have all been there. It's life. Jesus said, ***"In this life you will have trials and tribulations but know that I have overcome the world."*** If you abide in Jesus, He abides in you. And that means that there is an overcomer inside of you. So again, it's time to let go. The hurt is holding you back from the blessings coming your way. Drop the hurt and hope for the blessings.

QUESTIONS TO ASK SELF

1. What/Who do you need to let go of? What good do you gain from holding on to what is no longer there?

2. What do you need to forgive yourself for? What does forgiving yourself look like to you?

3. Who do you blame for your hurt? Are you still blaming that person for hurting you? What does it look like to let that hurt go?

4. Do you think that you are fully healed? If not, what else do you need to work through before you can say you are finally healed?

Focused

“Having anxiety and depression is like being scared and tired at the same time. It’s the fear of failure, but there is no urge to be productive.”

- RICK WILKERSON JR

Reflecting on my college experience one day in my senior year, I noticed a pattern. This wasn't a pattern that started in college but in high school. I realized that the environment I was in shaped the way I am now. I went to Collinwood High School, and if you know Collinwood, then you know it wasn't the best. Since the school academically wasn't great, there was no true academic challenge for us. Some teachers did strive to challenge our brains, but not many did. I am the type of person who, if I am not challenged, as mentioned earlier, would cruise through not putting total effort in. Having had this type of attitude for four years, it was easier for me to translate it to college. College students and graduates know that if you try to cruise through college, you will most likely be on your way to failure or dropping out. College academically was challenging, but I still had the same mindset from high school. Just do the bare minimum, and everything will work out. I can say that this worked for many classes. But from other courses, it did not. And when I say it left me stressed. I was fighting for my life. The classes that slapped me right in my face taught me a valuable lesson. The energy you sow will determine the reward you get in return.

I walked out with As and Bs in the classes I put total energy into. The classes that I didn't put energy into. We have a different story. I had some classes I unfortunately couldn't retake because they were Cs, and you can't retake classes you got Cs in and get a higher grade. What should have been a much higher GPA wasn't because I did the bare minimum. And doing the bare minimum comes with being a procrastinator. We've all held off doing something until the last minute. I always waited until the last minute to do the work because the bare minimum still got me to the finish line without recognizing it was a problem.

What ended up happening was that procrastination became my best friend. I didn't just procrastinate in school. I began to procrastinate spiritually, at work, and even with my gifts. Spiritually speaking, I thought praying before bed and waking up was enough, but it wasn't. I thought going to church every Sunday would be the anchor to staying connected to God, but it wasn't. I felt that reading at least one scripture daily would be enough, but it wasn't. Doing the bare minimum with God didn't set me up for what I longed for but pulled me further away from what I needed. I longed for a more intimate relationship with God, but I didn't get that because of my bare minimum attitude. I wanted to do more, but God can't use you publicly without working in private. I went from being a person who was one of the hardest workers to just going through the motions. And if you have ever just gone through the motions, you understand that feeling. It sucks!

I would best describe this state as waking up every day, doing the same thing, just checking the boxes that you did what was "needed." There's no excitement in waking up and looking towards the day ahead. You are already thinking about returning to bed when you get out—no enthusiasm for projects, work, or being around people. You are just there. Present in the body but far away mentally. You want to do more but are not allowing yourself to go deeper. You want to conquer all your tasks, but each day comes around, and you keep putting them off until tomorrow. It's how Rick Wilkerson Jr describes depression and anxiety. "Having anxiety and depression is like being scared and tired simultaneously. It's the fear of failure, but there is no urge to be productive." You're caught between wanting to be better and doing nothing. Wisdom tells you to do the work, but you do nothing. It's being trapped with the key in your hand to escape, but you sit there. You know what to do, but you are not doing it.

Around the time I was supposed to be studying for the LSAT, I wasn't because I had scored low the first time and was frustrated with myself. I knew that by studying, I would get better because I did before but didn't really study for months. My friend Deshaun would call me occasionally to ask me about it. I couldn't lie and tell him I was studying because it was written all over my face. (Face expressions are something I struggle with. I talk with my face all the time.) One day, he must have been fed up and kept it honest. "Why wait until tomorrow when you can get it done." I couldn't say anything to his comment because he was right. What was I doing at that moment was preventing me from studying? Why was I putting it off? Procrastination is birthed from the root of something. That something can be more than laziness. It may be fear of failure, lack of understanding, or tired of trying and not overcoming. I knew mine, and it was definitely all three of them.

EXPIRED BATTLE

While walking home from the gym one night, I continued conversing with God about what I had been having while working out. Midway through the conversation, I frustratedly uttered that I was tired of going through this. I didn't understand how I fought the same battle that started three years ago. Imagine fighting the same person for three years straight, and you still can't beat them. All moves were exposed during that time frame. Nothing should be catching you off guard, yet you still are losing. I had to ask God why I was still fighting this. His response baffled me. You're still fighting for two reasons. First, you haven't equipped yourself with the weapons to destroy your giant entirely. You knock the giant down to its knees but don't possess the weapon to take the kill shot. You leave the Giant room to regain strength, then come after you again. Secondly, you're not listening to the instructions I have already given you. When we pray, we ask God for signs and to speak to us. But the moment we get the sign or hear His voice, we turn from it. I remember God telling me once as I was about to ask Him for something, "I am not answering that because I have already given you the instructions on what to do."

Then the Holy Spirit spoke, "Stop asking God for the next, and you cannot even get through the now." When you have not killed your Goliath, there is no point in asking for the promised land. You have to kill Goliath before you can move ahead. When David killed Goliath, he did not kill him with the rocks he had. He took the knife out of the enemy's hand and used it to kill him. Take control of the tool the enemy is trying to kill you with, and you can kill them. The more I thought about it, the more it just made sense. There should be no reason why I couldn't find a way to defeat this for three years. I went to therapy, prayed, worshiped, and read my bible. Then why am I still down? I was using my rocks to knock the enemy out but wasn't taking the power out of the enemy's hand to finish my kill. I let the giant wake back up and come back for me. Three years is too long. I had all the understanding given to me by my therapist, preached words, and my personal bible study, but here I was, still struggling. I needed to lay this to rest, but how? That was my next question. What does finishing the kill look like?

This part takes some discipline, which I also fight with. It's about applying the given wisdom, which can become an internal war. We love learning to improve, but sometimes, our flesh speaks and pushes us back into our caves when it's time to do it. We become the ones stopping ourselves from growth. We think, "Maybe this is how I will always be," or "I'll always struggle with this," which gives our giants strength again. We talk ourselves out of walking in the newness of life that wisdom presented. It's the lie that sees us progressing that comes to slow us down. To finish our kill, we must declare not to go back and translate that into action, showing we are serious about not returning. Our giants cannot regain strength if our minds are immersed in the work. And that's when you know you have taken back the power. When you begin to follow the voice of wisdom, not the voice of the burden. The truth is that sin doesn't have control over us. Burdens that we carry, we don't have to carry them alone. We can trade our burdens with Jesus. (Matthew 11: 28-30).

YOU HAVE WHAT IT TAKE

As I mentioned, you have already been given the weapons to win this battle. Please don't take what I'm about to say personally. I've learned that you can't always talk to people a certain way because some are too sensitive. So, I always start with "I'm saying this out of love" when I am about to say something that can come off rude to others, but listen. Stop making excuses. Are you not tired of watching your life pass by? Are you not sick of feeling stuck? You have already been healed from what was bothering you. Yet, you are still here. God has already come and given you power over your enemy. However, you are still sitting here, acting like the enemy has authority over you. Get up!

Wipe the tears off your face. Stop asking God what to do. Please don't ask Him where He is. Don't ask Him when He will move on your behalf because God is already here, already moved, and is waiting on you. There is no more excuse to make. I'm sorry to tell you that. You have what it takes. You really do. You can step out on faith, or you can just let life pass you by doing nothing. The choice is up to you.

It doesn't matter if anybody else around you believes in you. If you do not believe in yourself, then there is no point in anybody else believing in you. Their belief in you can give you a little motivation, but for this to work, it depends on you. Not only do you have what it takes, but you must do whatever it takes. Whatever you have to do to return to peace. Do it! Whatever you have to do to return to a stable mindset. Do it! Do whatever it takes to reach your goals. Do what needs to be done to live out the calling over your life. Believe that you can do it. Believe that you have what it takes to overcome. Believe just like David believed when he faced Goliath. He believed that through the Almighty God, he would have victory. Fear cannot win. Get that through your head. The anxiety you are feeling right now cannot win. It won in the past, but do not let it succeed in the present.

Think about every trial you faced before. How many of those trials did you come out of on the winning side? All of them! Because nothing was made to break you but created to make you. So, what you see right now is a winnable fight if you believe you have what it takes. God will give you the second wind that you need. He will be your strength when you are weak. TD Jakes once said God cannot strengthen an "I" that won't do. So, be the "I" that does the work. Stand firm in full armor when He has you on the front line ready. Then you will see the victory, and finally, your giant will be placed under your feet. Get up! Get dressed! You have the power to win!

Stop Ignoring God

Feeling stuck can all be fixed by simple instructions. Obey. It's something that I can honestly say is a weak point for me. But it is also something that I can proudly say that I have been getting better at. I studied every person walking on purpose and wondered what got them there. After observing them and seeing what I was doing, I was convinced that obeying separated us. It had nothing to do with my anointing, drive, or gift. It was my inability to obey. Obey, or the word used in Deuteronomy 6, "Shema" means to hear and to do. As I studied this word, I was reminded of how I used to tell people, "I hear you," and then they would respond with, "But are you listening?". I didn't quite understand it then, but after studying this word, I now did. Hearing is not active. It takes nothing to hear; for a person who listens, it takes them to pay attention actively. Actively paying attention shows that you are devoted to what this person is saying and showing that you are not getting distracted by anything else.

Living in a world with so many distractions, we easily get caught up in not actively paying attention to God. If you sit here and tell me you never had a season where you weren't distracted, you would be lying to yourself. We have all been there and dealt with it. The struggle for focus has touched everybody. The good news is that God wants your focus back and will do what it takes to get you to focus on him, but are you ignoring God?

Your growth depends on how well you hear and do. Ignoring somebody isn't just zoning them out when they are talking to you. It also disregards what they are saying and keep doing whatever you please. You see this a lot in little kids. You can tell them not to touch that or not to do this, but the child might smile and then do it anyway. Their immaturity shows through their disobedience. In what area are you spiritually immature? Or yet, where are you the most disobedient? The place where you lack obedience is the place where you are full of immaturity. For you to grow up, you need to listen up. Hear what God is saying and do what He is saying. Don't think that God is ignoring you by not answering that prayer. It's you with the listening problem. What is it that you need to go back and do? What word did God give you that you know deep down inside that He is calling you to do? Whatever it is, go back and finish it. Only then will you have peace from the battle.

QUESTIONS TO ASK SELF

1. Does fear control you? How has fear stopped you from walking in purpose?

2. Are there any battles you feel like you should have overcome by now? Why are you still fighting the same battle? As you think over this, ask God to show you the weapons He has given you to overcome this giant once and for all.

3. Why have you been ignoring God? What would it look like if you started following God's voice more?

Don't Lose Hope

"Let your hope for the future speak louder than the pain of the past."

- Tavonne Bowman

So, I believe I mentioned it earlier, but most of this book was written while I was still in a season of suffering. Let me use a different word—a season of being crushed. While being crushed, I learned that I am a high-functioning, depressed person. High-functioning depression is being able to manage everyday life responsibilities while dealing with depression. A person who is high-functioning depressed may appear to the outside world fine, but on the inside, they are struggling. It is perceived that you are climbing every mountain with no problem, but they don't know that you are at your breaking point whenever something else happens. It seems you have it all together, but in reality, you feel like the pieces to the puzzle do not match at all.

I remember sitting in my friend circle, and one day, we decided to go around the room and say what we liked about each other. I remember it was Lyric's turn to go, and she spoke to me about my faith. She loved how strong I was in the faith, but when she told me that, my heart sank because I did feel that way. Not only did I feel that way, but what she or anybody else didn't see was that I was losing my faith. I wasn't losing my faith in the sense that now I was questioning if God was real. I was losing my faith in the sense that maybe God was done with me. Perhaps I'm not called anymore. It was my hope that it was going away and nobody noticed. And the only reason why people didn't see it was because high-functioning, depressed people roll with the punches. We fight the most emotional battles on the inside. Yet that doesn't stop us from getting out of bed and continuing with life.

Don't get it twisted. A high-functioning person still lacks motivation some days. We still think about quitting. We still wrestle in our minds. But the difference between us and major depressed people is that they may stay isolated for days, being chained mentally, doing absolutely nothing. Now, I am not bashing other depressed people who lock themselves in a room and don't come out. At this point, I want to push those who struggle worse than others to learn how to function better. I believe personal belief plays a part in the difference between high-functioning and major depression. High-functioning people walk through the stormy rain, hoping to see sunlight down the path. They expect, even when they feel like hope is pointless, that there is joy on the other side. Belief will do that to you. It will allow you to say, "I quit," but still show up the next day. It will make you take a 3-day break but return to see the project through. The hope that peace is coming pushes one to keep going.

For every major depressed person, I get your side of the story, though. Suppose I am honest, even though I call myself a high-functioning, depressed person. I, too, have felt hopeless. The Bible even points out that "hope deferred makes the heart sick." There is nothing worse than having a sick heart. Your heart is the center of everything. With your heart, you believe, think, love, and speak. Where a sickness occurs, a breakdown happens. If your heart becomes sick, everything else begins to break down. But it starts when hope is "crushed"

(Proverbs 13:12; GNT). Hope that is crushed is a deadly weapon.

It causes one to have depression, anxiety, and fear. It is the root of doubt. And it can even cause physical illness because sometimes people stop eating when their hope is crushed. People start to cope by drinking, smoking, or doing drugs. What hurts my heart is seeing people broken and stuck in a cycle because hope crushed the heart! And that's what we see with major depressed people. Dead on the inside, causing pain not only to self but to those who need them the most.

But hope is needed to keep pushing through. I hear you. The last time you put hope in something, it did not go your way. Trust me, I've been there and done that! But I know I can't have a vision if I don't have hope because hope allows me to dream about the future. And if you stop dreaming, you stop striving for the future. You cannot let what broke you in this season have authority over your ability to hope for the future. Your future needs you. What has happened is over with. And the truth is it happened for a reason. God doesn't do anything by accident but everything by design to paint a beautiful testimony about your life. So, when you are low in hope, turn to the God of Hope that will fill me with "joy and peace in believing" (Romans 15:13).

The God of Hope is the reason you can live on. What I love about God the most is that He sympathizes with our weaknesses and wants to know about what we go through. Not only that, but He wants to step into your problems. But it's on you to allow Him in! If you don't let your guard down for anybody else. Do yourself a favor and let your guard down for Him. You won't regret it, I promise. You will make the best life decision because you placed your expectations in the right place. See, you feel guarded and disappointed because you put your hope in man, not God.

When I changed where I put my hope, I was able to change my mind. When I shifted my thinking, I got back to work. I worked with the expectation that I got this. No, hope didn't free me from disappointment. Still, I would rather be disappointed trying than stand there disappointed that I let fear stop me from trying. I can't let the fear of disappointment win. If the fear of disappointment tells me not to try it, I can't listen. What if I come across an opportunity that will change my life? I wouldn't have gotten there if I had listened to the fear of disappointment.

I know it's hard because you have failed many times and are tired of failing. If I'm honest with you, I am too. I was exhausted from failing with relationships to the point that I gave up. But I know one day I will eventually want a wife and family. I'm tired of failing in my walk with Christ. But I cannot allow my failures to stop me from seeing what will come. And the only way I get that is to remind disappointment that I will and must overcome this! It takes courage to do that. It takes believing that the mess you see right now can be gone if you start cleaning it up. Let your hope for the future speak louder than the pain of the past.

THIS IS NOT THE END

This is not the end! What you are facing now will not take you out. I promise you that. You are stronger than you think. This all sounds like little clichés, but it is true. Just look at the last fight you were in. You won that fight. Your previous battle indicates that you have it in you to win again. Talking to my pastor one evening on the phone, she dropped an incredible gem. "Your private hells develop your public fire!". What you are facing privately was never meant to destroy you. It was always intended to produce the best you. Every punch you take, every storm you meet, every valley you walk through, and every hill you climb is intended to create a stronger you. A you that will be able to look back on this and say that it wasn't anything for real. You can help somebody in that same battle you are in now. You can give them the right weapons to fight with, the proper technique, and the right plan.

First, you have to remember that this is not the end. I've learned that the most potent motivator a person will need is themselves. There are a lot of gifted motivators out there that can make you ready to run through a brick wall, but only you can produce a fire inside of you that will prepare you to do the impossible. In this fight, you have to encourage yourself. David only succeeded against Goliath because he knew how to encourage himself. David faced bears and lions trying to eat the sheep when he tended the flock. For him to be still alive after that means that David encouraged himself and said, "This is not my ending." Personally, nine times out of ten, if I am face to face with a bear, I'm thinking this is it. But it takes a different type of self-talk to fight off a bear or lion, then turn around, look Goliath in the face (whom everybody else is afraid of), and tell him you are about to go down. But that's what encouraging yourself will do. And that's what belief in God looks like. Knowing He is fighting for and with you gives you a different confidence level to speak life into yourself.

It will give you the confidence to face your issue with no fear in your heart. You understand that the ending ends with glory when confidence invades your heart and mind. 1 Peter 5:10 says, "And after you have suffered a little while, the God of all grace, who has called you to his eternal glory in Christ, will himself restore, confirm, strengthen, and establish you." Your story is not over until you experience the restoration, confirmation, strengthening, and establishment of God. If the story did not come to the scene of those four stages, the story is not over. It has to end with you going through those four stages. That's where the ending is, not in the suffering but in the glory.

So, rejoice now! I know it's tough to do when you have not come out of your suffering, but God will make way for you. That's just who He is—a waymaking God. His name is El Roi. The God who sees me! He sees you, and he has not forgotten about you. He will show up for you. Just wait for Him. God comes at the right time, and I hate to say it, but His right time is not your suitable time. God sometimes waits until we are at our lowest points to show up. But I realized it's the lowest point of our lives where we finally surrender control. It's at the lowest point where we come to the conclusion that we give up. And that's what God wants. For you to

"Your private hells develop your public fire!".

give up control. As long as you try to be God in your life, He can't be God in your life. Surrender control and rejoice. Rejoice because you are in the Master's hands. It won't be long until you walk into your freedom. Get yourself together. Put your best outfit on, get your hair done, put on your best smell goods, and sit patiently. Your coming out party is about to take place!

Be aware of the so-called "Pharisees."

You're coming out party will have "Pharisees" there. The Pharisees in the Bible were always against Jesus. They dislike almost any and everything He did. From His teachings to His healing, they had a problem with it. On top of being against Jesus, the Pharisees were known to be religious leaders. Imagine that! Being religious but disliking the works of Jesus. I see it in today's society. Some people call themselves "Christians" but dislike it when they see somebody being healed. It irritates their soul when they see somebody who used to be one way but has changed. You have to be careful with them because these Pharisees will try to steal the joy that flows from the turnaround. Your freedom makes them cringe.

They enjoyed you as broken, so seeing you healed is something they never thought they would see. They don't like the fact you are put together. They don't like that they can't joke about your brokenness. Your transformation is not a miracle to them; it's an insult. Now that you have your peace and joy back, they think you are proclaiming to be better than them. But let them continue to believe whatever they want because their thoughts do not stop the hand of God over your life. God does not have to answer to the Pharisees. They have to answer to Him. And trust me, they will have questions, lies, and rumors ready to go when they see you free.

That's just how it goes. When I stopped doing the things I was doing, I had more people talking about me than I did before. It's like you were down with it when I said yes, but not that I'm turning away. It's an issue? And if I am honest, those types of people irritate my soul. I will be ready to go off on them, but I must remember that I can't approach the problem like that. Dealing with Pharisees, you cannot give them what they want. They want you to get out of character and respond. They want to have something to say about you. But in this restored season you are going into, you cannot give room to the enemy. Because once you give them what they want, they will think they have the power to chain you back up again. Let them talk, but don't give them the energy.

Allow God to be your Defender! That's something that I am learning to do, allowing God to fight the war while I sit back and shut up. It's easy for me to jump up and respond, but like I said, some things don't deserve the energy. And there have been rumors and lies that really made me furious, but I knew my reaction would be worse than the initial action. Leaning into the Defender helped me live in peace. The peace told me it doesn't matter what they say. The peace told me we know what the truth is. The peace reminded me that no matter how they may feel, God has not changed His mind about me!

Peace in that "vengeance is mine, says the Lord" (Romans 12:19). I could count on the Lord to be right there when they talked about me. He heard what they said just like I did, and He knows the right time to strike back. That's the beauty in it all. God sees and knows who hurts you. He will never let that judgment weight they put on you go unnoticed. He'll repay. I learned not to waste energy on foolishness because God will repay.

So, don't worry about those who talk about you. Don't let your hope for freedom disappear because some people want to keep you in bondage. Joseph was betrayed by his family. David's leader, Saul, did not want him to be promoted. The blind man was told to stop screaming for healing. Doctors manipulated the woman with the issue of blood was manipulated for 12 years. The prodigal son's brother hated that he was celebrated for returning home. And Jesus!? Jesus was talked about. He was lied on, backstabbed, forgotten, and betrayed by His friends. He was beaten, spit on, and not even respected in His hometown. Yet, none of the adversity any of these people faced ever stopped the purpose of their lives. God still completed the work in His people. Christ still completed His mission. Despite the struggle, depression, stormy days, and no place to lay His head. And so can you! This is your sign to live on despite the hell you are in. Live on! Much love.

QUESTIONS TO ASK SELF

1. Why are you afraid to hope again? Has God ever failed you? If not, why haven't you put your faith in Him? What distractions is blocking your faith lens?

2. Are you ready to quit? How can you convince yourself that this is not the end?

3. How does your belief in God help you to overcome depression?

YOU ARE LOVED, YOU ARE CHOSEN, AND YOU WILL BE GREAT BECAUSE OF THE GREAT I AM THAT LIVES IN YOU. DAYS WHEN YOU WANT TO QUIT, LET THE FRUSTRATIONS OUT. TIMES WHEN YOU WANT TO DIE, REMEMBER YOUR PURPOSE, AND IF YOU DON'T KNOW YOUR PURPOSE, ASK YOURSELF WHAT AM I PASSIONATE ABOUT? AND THERE IS WHERE YOU FIND YOUR PURPOSE. NEVER LET GO. NEVER GIVE UP. IT'S OKAY NOT TO BE OKAY. IT'S OKAY TO TAKE BREAKS. THIS IS A LONG JOURNEY. YOU ARE ALLOWED TO REST, BUT REMEMBER THIS ONE PHRASE FOR ME. "IF SUICIDE EVER CROSSES YOUR MIND, JUST KNOW I WOULD RATHER LISTEN TO YOUR STORY THAN ATTEND YOUR FUNERAL." I WILL BE YOUR LISTENING EAR! TO THOSE WHO COMMITTED SUICIDE, WE WISH YOU WERE STILL HERE. WE MISS YOU, AND WE APOLOGIZE FOR NOT UNDERSTANDING YOU.

TILL WE MEET AGAIN